A DISCOURSE

CONCERNING SOME EFFECTS OF THE

LATE CIVIL WAR

ON

Ecclesiastical Matters

IN KENTUCKY,

Delivered in the Hall of the City Library, Lexington, Kentucky, on

Sunday, November 13th, 1866.

BY L. L. PINKERTON, M.D.

CINCINNATI:
A. MOORE, BOOK AND JOB PRINTER, 230 WALNUT STREET.
1866.

To the memory of Marshall Headly, late of Allendale, Jessamine county, Kentucky, I dedicate the following discourse. Between him and the writer there was a substantial agreement on all the great issues of the civil war and especially on the subjects treated in the address, which were often and, anxiously discussed, during the last year of his life.

A thoughtful man, but never in haste to speak, he incessantly pondered in his heart the great issues of the terrible conflict, and though sorrowful always, and at times desponding, he never faltered in stern loyalty to his government, nor to his race; or in fealty to his Saviour.

Of ample fortune, yet despising the social consideration which men are too apt to claim on that ground alone, he was, to the last, the friend and intimate companion of the poorest of men.

Making no pretension to learning, his knowledge of men, of society, and of all the graver affairs of human life, was wide, intimate and accurate. His habit of uttering the most matured opinions in the interrogative form, as though he would inquire rather than affirm, did not conceal from his intimate friends, his just confidence in the general correctness of the conclusions he had reached.

In the constant exercise of a most generous hospitality, and though in the Fifty-ninth year of his age, he had the happy faculty of making himself agreeable to the young of both sexes, and his usually quiet, country home, was, for them, a chosen place of gathering. Alas! we shall see him on earth no more. At a time when we expected it not—in July, 1866, the Destroyer came, and our cherished, most constant friend passed away.

Our sorrows may be soothed by the firm belief that another tired spirit has found rest in heaven, and we may seek to assuage our grief by the hope of meeting him there, when the dream of life is past; but we shall not think of our great loss without sighing, nor cease to feel that for our riven hearts there is no perfect healing this side the tomb.

Farewell "Marshall." The remains of men have been followed to the grave by more weepers than followed thine, but none by truer, sadder hearts, and of those bleeding hearts, few were *more* hopelessly crushed than was his, who now lays this humble, but tear-hallowed tribute of affection on thy grave.

REMARKS.

The style of the following discourse is obnoxious to criticism, which, however, is not particularly deprecated. Graceful utterance was not to be thought of, had the writer possessed taste and talent for it. The aim of the discourse required that the *argument* should be brief and its applications numerous and *direct*. Allusions to local circumstances were indispensable. Indeed, the utility of the discourse, if it shall prove to be of any, depends upon these allusions, although they can scarcely be intelligible to those not acquainted with the course of religious events in Kentucky, during and since the close of the late civil war.

It is known to all, that early in the year 1863, a large portion of the slave-holding element in the "loyal party" of Kentucky, dissented so far from the "policy of the Administration in regard to slavery," that they deemed it expedient to denounce the government openly, and even furiously. In ordinary times, thoughtful men find no difficulty in discriminating between a government, and any existing administration of that government, but in the actual state of affairs in Kentucky in 1863, such discrimination was *practically* impossible. Men can not walk a slack-rope in the midst of a hurricane. It is believed that every candid and enlightened "rebel" will admit, that this class of "union men," was, *in effect*, co-operants of the insurgents, from the beginning of the year 1863, till the close of the war. Many, certainly, did not *intend* this result, while others, as was natural, threw off all pretense of "loyalty," and became avowed "rebels." Now I wish to say most distinctly, that though I think many of these "Union men" committed a serious blunder, I have no harsher word to say of them.

A very earnest desire has been entertained not to give offense to any sincere, well-meaning persons, who may be included in the classes deemed censurable for complicity in the gravest crimes. Possibly, however, after all the care that could be bestowed in that direction, some expressions may be found, that had better been omitted. It is possible too, that almost unconsciously, I may have felt something bordering on resentment towards those who have, during almost six years, malevolently and persistently misrepresented my sentiments, misinterpreted my actions, and invented and circulated the most scandalous falsehoods, to my great injury. I have endeavored to hold in abeyance every remembrance of *personal* wrong endured, and every sentiment of indignation; and if I have not succeeded fully, those will be readiest to forgive, whose nobleness of nature renders them fit to appreciate the difficulty of such a preformance.

Having tried to be faithful to my country in the hour of her calamity, having endeavored to do what appeared to be my duty toward the colored race, having sought to be true to the teachings of the Bible, and to what I thought to be the "great principles of the Reformation," I stand in the midst of relentless enemies, undismayed, determined to do and dare to the last. The fight with frost and famine, daily growing more urgent, is far preferable to the surrender of truths, on the support of which, as it seems to me, depends the existence of our civilization, and the progress of mankind.

If those Christians who agree with me in the importance of the principles contended for, shall yet prefer to give aid to those who have practically denied and deserted those principles, they will but furnish another sad illustration of the weakness and inconsistency of which men are capable. "In God we trust."

December 14*th*, 1866.

DISCOURSE.

"Truth faileth, and he that departeth from evil maketh himself a prey; and the Lord saw it, and it displeased him that there was no judgment."—Isaiah, lix. 15.

Truth, eternal and divine truth, is, indeed, the pearl of great price. It is the only food ordained of Heaven for the sustenance and growth of the immortal mind. Falsehood and error are essentially negative; they are and yet are not, and shall ultimately go into perdition.

The love of truth *for its own sake*—truth in respect of everything which is a subject of human thought, or that in any way connects itself with the affairs and fortunes of the human race, we may safely regard as among the chief evidences of spiritual enfranchisement. They in whom abides evermore a supreme and trembling reverence for truth, have, we may be assured, passed from death unto life. On the other hand, we might infer, even in the absence of specific Bible teaching, that he who disregards truth, is not of God. By truth is not here meant religious or theological truth exclusively, but any and all truth.

It is quite possible for any man to mistake his way in seeking after truth, even when the search is conducted earnestly and with entire singleness of aim. This should suggest caution, deliberation, patience, in the prosecution of our inquiries; the holding in abeyance of all selfish, partizan purposes and aims; and, except in cases which admit of demonstration, or which appeal directly to the moral intuitions, our liability to error, will justify diffidence, and condemn dogmatism, with respect to the results of our investigations. Notwithstanding liability to error, and admitting whatever charities and proprieties the fact may demand, still, there are truths about which, among sane people, there can be no difference of opinion; and it is the observance and the advocacy of these truths that determine a man's moral status. The man, for instance, who would seriously question the equity of the "Golden Rule"—"Whatever you would that men should do to you, do ye even so to them," is simply an idiot or a knave. It has been truly observed by a distinguished writer, that for us, for all men, there exist ineradicable distinctions among things, as good and bad, right and wrong, true and false. We can not rid ourselves of the conviction that these distinctions are not conventional, but real, and that our characters ought to be determined by means of these distinctions. The man who is not *true to his own convictions* of what is good and right and true, is himself a falsehood in God's universe, let his pretensions be what they may, and in his own consciousness, he is aware of the humiliating fact. He who is false to his convictions of truth and right, is false utterly, and puts out the light that is in him; and we all of us know who uttered the fearful words,—"If the light that is in you be darkness, how great is that darkness!" The immense importance of this subject—its fundamental relation to pure morals and true religion, and to the true and hoped-for social state, must be my apology for dwelling upon it. Let us then appeal to the sacred Scriptures.

"Because they received not *the love of the truth*, that they might be saved, God shall send them strong delusion that they should believe a lie, that they all might be damned, who believed not the truth, but had pleasure in unrighteousness." 2 Thes., ii 10, 11.

This is a terrible declaration, my brethren, instinct with the wrath of God. I have no time for its unfolding and application, but we may be assured that in this matter of truth, God will not be trifled with; and he who sets himself to oppose what, in his heart, he knows to be right and true, will end by believing a lie. Nor does this take place by the interposition of miracle, but in strict harmony with the laws of our intellectual and moral nature.

Among the qualifications for standing before God in Mount Zion, is this; that a man shall "speak the truth *in his heart;*" that is, he shall be unwaveringly true to his convictions. Psalmn 15. The Savior of the world, who came forth from the bosom of the Father, declares himself to be the way and *the truth* and the life; while, on the other hand, he says of the great adversary, the Devil, that "he was a murderer from the beginning and abode not in the truth, because there is no truth in him. When he speaks a lie, he speaks of his own, for he is a liar and the father of it." John, viii, 44. "Whoever loves or makes a lie," is classed by the Holy Spirit with the most abominable characters known on earth or in hell; and finally, the Scriptures declare that "all liars shall have their part in the lake that burns with fire and brimstone, which is the second death."

I have thought it well, on many accounts, to refer to these declarations of God's word; and surely in view of these, to which we might add indefinitely, it becomes every one to seek the truth with his whole heart, and to abide in it; to "buy the truth and sell it not," while he shuns falsehood, as he would shun the gates of hell. Do we judge harshly in supposing that these times of ours render the reference we have made to the Bible, specially appropriate? Are men now, generally seeking the truth, or what they suppose to be their private interests? Do they demand, even in the church, sincerity and honesty, or acquiescence?

I shall continue to assume, in this address, that the Bible is true in its own sense; that is to say, it contains a revelation of God's will concerning the human race; that this will is the highest law to every human being to whom it comes, and that ignorance or disregard of it, so far at least as duty is involved, is fatal. No Christian will question the supreme obligation of every one to use all diligence to ascertain the exact meaning of God's law; nor will any one doubt that habitual, persistent disregard of its teachings, involves infinite peril. We may add, that ingenious perversions of the sacred Scriptures, or sophistical evasions of their obvious import, is of the very quintessence of sin. Indeed, we judge that it would be every way better to remain in wilful ignorance of God's word, or knowing its teachings, boldly to disregard and defy them, than to attempt to make Jehovah a co-partner in our sins, by so wresting his revelation as to make it testify in favor of iniquity.

An additional remark must be allowed, even if it should be ranked among pulpit platitudes. No man can afford to incur the wrath of Almighty God, because *no man can afford to lose his soul.* Any thing that can be achieved or imagined is preferable to this. It is the consummation of all possible calamities. Death by slow fire or lingering starvation, would be agreeable entertainment compared with an abode in "outer darkness where the worm dieth not, and the fire is not quenched." "Fear not them," said Jesus, "who can kill the body, but after that can do no more, but fear him who, having killed the body, can destroy both soul and body in hell; yea, I say unto you, fear him. It is a fearful thing to fall into the hands of the living God." On the other hand, all of honor and glory and bliss and blessdeness, that is possible to a finite being, shall be given of God to him who abides in the truth. Hence, to accept heartily the divine teaching, and to follow it at all costs, even unto death, is not mearly duty, religion, it is sound discretion as well. If the expression may be allowed "it pays" infinitely, and this alone, of all the enterprises in which one can engage in this world does "pay." To all who fail in fealty to truth and to God, life will, at the last, prove an infinite misfortune—it "were better for such had they never been born." We would thus indicate the spirit and temper in which our investigations are to be this day conducted.

Why, then, are we here to day? We are here to bear witness to the truth,—we are here to do and to suffer, if need be, for the word of God, and the testimony of Jesus; we are here because God's people have sinned greviously without rebuke, because they have participated in, connived at, and applauded the most monstrous crimes known to the laws of God and to the laws of man—we are here to discharge our most solemn duties to our brethren, to our country, and to our race, the whole being our bounden duty to Him who gave himself a ransom for our forfeited souls. We neither intend nor invite schism, but we intend to assert and to enjoy our inalienable rights, whether as citizens of the state, or of the kingdom of God. We intend to exercise our right to announce the *whole* counsel of God, as His infinite providence may open for us a door of utterance.

For the present, we have no judgement to pronounce upon those without the pale of the church. As a public teacher of religion, we have nothing to say of them, at any time, but to preach to them as we may be able, "the glorious gospel of the blessed God." To the church, our mission is different. Here, we are to reprove, rebuke and exhort, with all long-suffering, when in our convictions, it becomes our duty so to do; nor dare we employ craftiness, nor "handle the word of God deceitfully." We may remark further, that our present business is with that church of which the speaker has been a member for more than thirty-six years—for more than twenty-eight, a public minister. What cause we may have for protest, for rebuke, for reproof, are now to be briefly stated and argued.

No precepts of the Bible are plainer or more explicit than these, namely: "That Christians shall obey magistrates; that they shall submit themselves to the regularly constituted civil authorities of the countries in which they may reside, whatever may be the forms in which that authority shall be expressed. "Whoever resisteth the civil power, resisteth *the ordinance of God*, and they that resist shall receive to themselves damnation." Civil or *political* rulers are God's ministers. Romans xiii. We intend no elaborate argument—it is not called for. The Christian who, as such, denies his obligation to obey the Civil rulers of his country, would deny his obligation to pay his debts. When the civil authorities contravene the authority of Heaven, it is not questioned that the latter is to be obeyed. No such emergency having arisen in this country, this phase of the general subject is not now under discussion; nor are we now required to discuss the right of Christian men to rebel against despotic rulers. It will be time enough to discuss the latter subject when a necessity for it shall arise. We but express, however, the universal sense of the civilized world in saying, that armed revolution or insurrection is always an extreme, even a desperate remedy for political evils, and can not be lawfully resorted to till all peaceful means of redress shall have been tried without effect. But in a government shaped and directed by constitutional majorities, *and whose organic law provides for its own change by such majorities*, all pretext for insurrection is barred wholly and forever. Insurrection, under such state of case is utterly inexcusable, wanton and wicked. Now, we charge first, that just such an insurrection did thousands of Christian people in Kentucky raise, prosecute, and encourage against the lawful "powers" of the United States, and against the direct authority of Jesus Christ, commanding them to be subject to these very powers "for conscience sake." Romans xiii, 5.

We charge, in the second place, that these erring people of God, prosecuted this insurrection for a period of four terrible years, and that they signalized the revolt by deeds of unparalelled atrocity—of more than barbaric cruelty. Almost every crime known to the Decalogue was committed to an appalling extent, as a direct consequence of the war, and all of which is to be charged to those who instigated, encouraged or approved the revolt.

We do not purpose to recite the events of 1860 in proof of the utter wickedness of our late rebellion; but we believe it susceptible of the clearest and most overwhelming proof that a more reckless and inexcusable insurrection against a benignant and free government, or against any government, has not been waged since the making of the world. Even if we allow the assigned reason for the rebellion to have existed namely, that the perpetuity and extension of African slavery were menaced by the majority of the nation, the reason itself is of so questionable a character as might well cause a Christian to pause long and prayerfully ere he called to arms. What was African Slavery in the United States, that Christians should rush into war in its support? Were its indefinite duration and extension to be desired? Was the *natural* right of five hundred thousand white men to compel and to appropriate the labor of four millions of black men, quite clear to Christ's disciples? Were the *unavoidable* concomitants of slavery such as to commend it to the children of God? Were the ignorance and social and moral degradation intrinsically incident to the institution, calculated to win the favor of those in whom dwells the spirit of Christ? Let the honest man lay his hand upon his heart, and with eyes raised to heaven, answer. God will one day compel him and all men to answer. But even the poor plea for the rebellion, that slavery was endangered by the political events of 1860, can not be allowed; for thousands of those most deeply interested in the perpetuity and extension of slavery, and of these, many best able to judge, scouted the plea as idle and frivolous. Therefore the insurrection was utterly without justification; for, if the pretext for it was such as a Christian dare avow at the bar of Jesus, still, even that pretext was feigned. With candid and well-informed people, it were useless to argue this matter; with the ignorant and those reckless of truth, it would be useless.

But we have said that this insurrection, raised professeply for the extension and perpetuation of the bondage of four millions of human beings for whom the son of God died—the bondage of four millions and their posterity, together with all the ignorance and degradation inseparable from that bondage—was accompanied by deeds of peculiar and appalling atrocity. There were interludes in the awful drama, in harmony with its avowed object, and which served as infallible exponents of the chief actors. The subject is an unpleasant one at any time, and we have no desire to enter into details.

We shall instance only the destruction of, at least, twenty thousand young men by slow starvation in pens in which, even mules would have died by the thousand under like treatment; and the deliberate murder, at one time, of several hundred prisoners of war, in the most cruel and savage manner.

Now, what we demand is, that God's people shall acknowledge the sin and shame of this unholy insurrection, and that they shall denounce the unnecessary and shocking cruelties that accompanied it; or, if it can be made to appear that both the great parties to the war are alike guilty before God, let both be denounced in the name of humanity, in the name of religion, in the name of the Lord. That one or the other party has fearfully sinned, none can doubt. Let the erring children of God, then, be rebuked and called to repentance, and let the word of the Lord go forth against all ungodliness and unrighteousness of men, who hold the truth in unrighteousness.

So far, however, are Christian "rebels" from repentance for having levied war against their lawful rulers, that they justify themselves in it,—they avow that they did right in the sight of God and man. Dare we concede this, even tacitly? Dare we allow that a war of four years duration—a war that has alienated friends; that has made the taking of oaths, to an alarming extent, the merest mockery, and perjuries almost as numerous as collisions between rebel and loyal interests—that has burdened a nation with an incalculable debt—that by enhancing the price of food and fuel and clothing, has caused immense privation and suffering among the poor; that left general desolation in its track over large districts of our country; that has left behind it tens of thousands of darkened and broken homes, and millions of broken hearts; that has scattered hundreds of thousands of maimed and crippled men over a continent, and that sent half a million to bloody graves—can we allow, that without incurring terrible guilt, such a war may be levied and encouraged by Christ's disciples against a beneficent government, and in the interests of human bondage? If so, our notion of sin is a delusion—the gospel a cunningly devised fable.

If we have been able to understand, even to a small extent, the relations of the Christian ministry to the church and to general society, nay, if we rightly apprehend the providential calls of God, then has he made it the special *present* duty of his ministers to call his erring people to repentance for their participation in the greatest crimes. Such is, in our judgment, the "burden" of Kentucky,—the duty of this day, for those who stand before her people in the name of Jesus and for the souls of men.

That an overwhelming majority of these ministers should themselves tacitly, or by open avowal, justify the great rebellion in the interests of such an institution, as they know African slavery to have been, is among the most startling and discouraging facts connected with that rebellion. It would be pleasant to hope that they have been guided in their reasonings by the spirit of Him who was sent to proclaim liberty to the captives; the opening of the prison doors to them that were bound; to break *every* yoke, and to proclaim the accepted year of the Lord. We should willingly believe that these ministers have not been swayed in their judgments by the circumstance that, since the beginning of the year 1863, a very large majority of the wealthy people of Kentucky, the slaveholders—have been heartily or virtually on the side of insurrection and a divided nation. Most certainly no such unanimity among the ministers of our state on any "political" question was ever before witnessed. It is remarkable, *very* remarkable. Watchmen! What of the night? With pallid lips and bated breath you glide silently about among sins that fill the whole earth, and darken the sun and heaven—sins that bode the overthrow of government, of church and of civilization together. Have you lost faith in God and in your own souls? In the truth of God and in the consciences of men? And if one of your brethren should believe himself moved of God to raise his voice against "lawlessness," and in behalf of *what you know* to be the natural, inalienable rights of man, you stand quietly by while the mob cries crucify him; or doubtfully and gravely shaking your reverend heads, you coolly question your brother's sanity. But you are prudent, you say. It is, perhaps, well when we can persuade ourselves, that what in others would be considered time-serving policy, in ourselves, is only Christian prudence. Pilate was "prudent," doubtless, when, awed by popular clamor, and yet stung by conscience, he asked of Jesus, "*what is truth*," but waited no reply.

> "Dissolved the court and mingled with the throng,
> Asylum sad, from reason, hope and heaven."

But you are "prudent"—are you consistent? You can cry aloud against the sin of dancing; you can declaim long and earnestly against "instrumental music in churches:" you can "deal damnation round the land," against good men and women, who, at the very worst, have only mistaken the meaning of a Greek word; but for those who commit perjury; for those who refuse to hear and obey the voice of God in relation to their duties to the civil rulers; for those who perpetrate or applaud the greatest crimes, you have no word of rebuke! But you are "prudent" men. Yes, verily, you *are* prudent, and right well does your prudence pay.

It becomes sinners, whose only refuge is the mercy of God, to judge one another tenderly; and yet, we are wholly unable to see any thing in this boasted "prudence," other than the tithing of herbs, while the weightier matters of the law, justice, mercy, and the fear of God are neglected. That any sane man believes it to be more heniously sinful in the sight of God to dance, or to use an organ in the public worship, than to take up arms and inaugurate war against a free, constitutional government, we shall believe, when we shall see a man swallow a camel, and then choke on a gnat.

The reply to our suggestions is stereotyped,—" We want no mingling of politics with religion—we want no politics in the pulpit." So we say, and with all possible emphasis. Let us have no homilies on finance, free trade, internal improvement, reconstruction, the right of suffrage, the boundaries of Executive, Legislative, or Judicial authority, States rights, etc., etc.; (*but let no man call God's word politics.*) We say nothing here on the right or the necessity of secession in 1861; but we do say, that according to the plain teaching of the New Testament, the disciples of Christ who engaged directly or indirectly in the late insurrection against the government of the United States, are guilty before God of the gravest crimes.

The relation of the American pulpit to civil affairs calls for calm and thorough discussion; meanwhile, we might well suppose that those in Kentucky who protest most earnestly against "political preaching," would be a little cautious in their denunciations. Did their co-operants in rebellion in the South, hesitate to "preach politics" before or during the war? For years the southern pulpits rung with the glory and divinity of Slavery, and the right of revolution. Gov. Perry, of South Carolina, charges the late civil war mainly to three classes—politicians, editors and ministers; and our recollection is, that he gives the preeminence in the bad work to the ministers. They did certainly employ their fervid eloquence during the war, to fan the sectional prejudices of their people into a flame, and to keep them burning. Even some of those ministers who went from Kentucky to the South or to Canada during the war, did not hesitate to speak for Slavery and the rebellion there, *and for secession before their departure.* We have, besides, conclusive evidence, that however averse some Kentucky Christians may now be to having the pulpit profaned by what they falsely call political preaching, they would have been easily reconciled to the profanation, had Gen. Bragg held the State for the "Southern Confederacy." Hopeful beginnings were made in that direction, even during his short stay with us in 1862. More recently, too, some of these anti-political preachers found it convenient and expedient, and no doubt "*prudent*," to signalize with religious services, the exhumation and re interment of the remains of certain guerrillas, executed under military order, in retaliation for the murder of peaceful citizens. Allusion is made to these matters with extreme reluctance, but under an irrepressible conviction of duty. He who fails to see that the expressed horror of political preaching among us, is shallow affectation — is easily deceived. It is a device of Satan to spike the artillery of God. Away with it! The faithful minister must declare the whole counsel of God, though it condemn himself and his hearers together. He must, for instance, expound the teaching of the Bible in relation to matrimony, when the time shall come, even through a political party, to secure the vote of Utah, shall declare itself in favor of polygamy, and other domestic and social abominations of Mormonism. No doubt, such minister will be duly denounced as a political preacher. In a word, "Whatever things are true, whatever things are honest, whatever things are just, whatever things are pure, whatever things are lovely, whatever things are of good report," within the meaning and purpose of God's word, are not only legitimate themes of pulpit discussion, but the minster of Jesus Christ is solemnly bound to teach and to enforce them, and to oppose and to rebuke whatever is opposed to them, whether the things so opposed be political or not.

But in the third place: the Christian people, to whose course we have taken exception, not only took part in a most unrighteous war,—not only have they approved or excused the needless enormities which characterized it, but they have proscribed, maligned and persecuted every preacher whose views of duty to his country, to his race, and to his Redeemer, caused him resolutely and uncompromisingly to oppose the rebellion and to actively aid his constitutional government—and this, nothwithstanding *such preachers may not have spoken one word pro or con, in the pulpit, on the subject of the war, from its beginning till its close.*

The reply is—"Loyal men are not proscribed. A. B. C. and D. are loyal, and no one objects to their preaching." These "loyal" brethren, who are acceptable to rebel churches, have, most likely, thought it "prudent" not to vote since the year 1860; and in general, their whole course in relation to the war, did much more in aid of the insurrection, than for the salvation of an imperilled nation. They have found it "prudent" to condemn "whatever was wrong on both sides," taking special care to say about as much against the one party as against the other.

Discerning rebels understood the policy of this class of men, and availed themselves of their effective co-operation. Preachers, who, since 1863, have spoken no harsh word of the rebellion, not even condemning Andersonville and Fort Pillow, but who, during the same time, have heaped upon the United States government and those who upheld it, every opprobrium, might well be acceptable to "rebels." As things actually were in Kentucky, they were able to do more, and did more for the rebellion, than the original secessionists. A few of these "loyal preachers," have recovered their standing by simply denouncing the Missouri preachers' oath. Tired of social and ecclesiastical ostracism, they eagerly availed themselves of that opening to the hearts of those whom their loyalty had offended. They have found their reward.

"It is only the decided, out-spoken loyal preachers,—those who voted and otherwise showed a deep interest in the results of the war, that we proscribe," say some. In reply, we ask a single question: Do these brethren condemn equally, those who *preached* secession in Kentucky during the war, and who, leaving the State for Canada or the Confederacy, preached openly there in behalf of slavery, secession, and rebellion? What shocking insincerity must the answer to this question disclose? We forbear to press it. It might be well for the parties involved to remember, that "an unjust balance is an abomination to the Lord." It is very clear to all, that the hostility of our "rebel" brethren to "preachers who dabble in politics," is determined altogether by the kind of politics in which they "dabble."

We ask then, further, that Christians shall at once cease to persecute and proscribe loyal ministers, and that they no longer visit the alleged sins of loyal fathers upon the heads of their innocent women and children. We demand also, that ministers who can neither be coaxed nor bribed into silence concerning the sin of the late rebellion, shall be allowed, as well as the "prudent" and the disloyal ministers, to occupy the pulpits, and to preach to all who may wish to hear them, according to their own convictions of duty and propriety. To this proposition the reply would be: "Such proceedings would result in division." Indeed! And is Christian union then to be maintained by inhibiting the discussion of any grave question about which there may exist differences of *faith*. What is such union worth?

It would be well, meanwhile, on many accounts, for some of those who seem willing to ignore whole sections of the New Testament, in order to secure harmony in churches, to call to mind the former times. The Baptists of Kentucky, forty years ago, held, or were supposed to hold, an erroneous theory of conversion, and to have failed in their apprehension of the design of Christian baptism, and of some other matters, more or less clearly revealed in the Bible. Did our "Reformers" of that day, some of whom still survive, hesitate to preach *their* views of conversion and baptism, *lest the Baptist churches should be divided?* The legs of the lame are not equal. By the persistent preaching of "the *views* of the Reformers,"—and that, not in the mildest and most winning tone—perhaps half the Baptist churches in Kentucky *were* divided; and this too, notwithstanding the Baptists were then and are now, regarded as Christians by those who caused their division. "But, then, the 'Reformers' preached the truth." Be it so. Is not the 13th chapter of Romans truth? and does it not convict all Christians who *willingly, in any way, and to any extent*, participated in the late insurrection against the United States, of most heinous sin against God? Have the Baptist theories, right or wrong, resulted in great evil to society. It is, doubtless, well for us all, that the grace of God which brings salvation, is not circumscribed by our theological diagrams. The Baptists are still with us, and like the rest of us, with their good and their not-good, are struggling fairly abreast of other Christian people, for the "crown of righteousness." Peace be with them, and with the Israel of God.

But "the Reformers preach the truth." Be it so, we still reply; and is not this truth—"Whatever ye would that men should do to you, do ye even so to them"? and has this any conceivable application to our treatment of our late slaves, who are here and free, by no agency of their own? What have we even *attempted* to do for their conversion to God—their elevation to higher planes of spiritual life, and of social life among themselves? Some who have feebly attempted this, have been denounced, shunned, maligned; others have been mobbed, without any voice of protest from any pulpit in the State. Meeting houses have been refused, that were otherwise unused, that these poor people might not be instructed in the duties incident to their changed condition. In the meantime, no discussion of any matter, nor any allusion to any matter, that can possibly disturb the equanimity of those who desired the destruction of the nation, and who still desire its destruction, is to be tolerated. Such is the decision of "the elders." And this is Christian union, alas! It may be a league with Death and a covenant with Hell, but Christian union, it is not. Besides, *it is a loud, practical, and despotic protest against the most fundamental principle of the "Reformation."* And do those erring people of God, who thus protest, expect permanently to hold in abeyance, the discussion of great questions that lie at the very basis of all morality? As well attempt to stop an eruption of Vesuvius with a handful of feathers, as to arrest discussion by the cry of "division in churches." Churches that refuse to hear the truth of God, need not fear division, nor even annihilation—something much more to be dreaded than either, or both, impends.

If we have read history to any purpose, we have learned that great social revolutions are preceded and followed by discussions of great principles—principles that lie at the foundations of states and of churches. This is an ordination of Providence by which progressive nations advance to higher levels of intellectual, social and moral life. Let us, then, have full and free discussion, conducted in meekness and gentleness, in a spirit of forbearance and long-suffering; and let the word of the Lord prevail—"yea, let God be true, and every man a liar."

One plea often urged in vindication of the rebellion, is of so remarkable a character, as to demand a passing notice. Were it not presented by men "professing godliness," we should regard it as simply the offspring of irreverent, if not blasphemous unbelief. "You of the loyal party," those "men of God," are accustomed to say, "regard the *results* of the rebellion as salutary. Slavery is abolished, at least, and for this, you ought to be thankful to those who inaugurated and carried on the insurrection." On the same ground, then, the chief priests and elders, who *through envy*, accused the Saviour of the world before Pilate, and even Pilate himself, who through fear of the mob, wrested judgment, and "delivered Jesus to be crucified," are entitled to the gratitude of the human race! Could a more appalling illustration of the danger of trifling with truth be found, than this case presents? It is the prerogative of an infinite and merciful Providence, to make the wrath of man to praise him, while he restrains the remainder; it is His to bring good out of evil, and thus prevent our race from rushing at once upon irremediable ruin; but of him who shall, on this account, make a merit of sin, and claim the right to "do evil that good may come," an Apostle declares, that "his damnation is just."

The seeds of all that is most conservative,—of all that is best in American civilization, crossed the ocean in the Mayflower; that is to say, an unflinching faith in the Bible, as being a revelation of God's will to man, and as containing the rule of the final judgment that is to be passed upon every individual of the human race, by the Creator himself. We may deride, if we will, this stern faith of the Puritans, their confidence, of the old Hebrew type, in the providence of God; we may make ourselves merry over their "grave and exaggerated piety," but as our people recede from what was *central* in their faith, to that extent do they render insecure their liberties, whether civil or religious. We steadfastly believe that our cherished liberties can be assured but in one way, and that is, by the faithful exhibition of the morality and religion of the Bible, by means of a faithful living ministry, and by the press. We should be thankful, that the most sacred duties of the ministry, are concurrent with the dictates of the loftiest and purest patriotism. Without Protestant Christianity, in its *most distinctive elements*, we may have something like an exaggerated Mexico, or a French Republic, but the great, free Republic of America, we can not have. The foundation of Protestantism is the Bible, including the 13th chapter of Romans,—and nothing but the Bible, fairly interpreted and applied, in all its vast range, to all the serious affairs of human life, domestic, social, political,—the application of its principles and explicit statutes to every question of human duty and privilege. We may apply to our own beloved country, what a great writer, Isaac Taylor, has so eloquently said of England:

"To a community within which the gospel has widely diffused itself, through the opinions, habits and affections of the mass, and in which it intensely affects the moral energies of thousands, the ceasing to be Christian would be a dissolution, political, social, domestic: it would be—national death.

"In this country, every institution that now fortifies and adorns our social condition, has been constructed on the supposition of a flow and pressure in one direction; that is, toward what is, or is assumed to be true in religion and pure in morals—every slope in the political building is adapted to this and to no other movement of the waters—should they turn, there is not an embankment which must not yield, and add its fragments to the general ruin. America and her affluence at home and her influence throughout the world, and her bright cluster of honors; America and her pure domestic affections and her home felicities; her generous temper and her wide philanthropy; America and her power and her embellishments, we may be assured, is fated along with the gospel. The waters of the sanctuary stand breast high around her, and should they fall off, she herself falls to rise no more."

These are significant words, and if we experiment recklessly with our duties as citizens, to our cost, we shall find them prophetic. Indeed, my brethren, I can not regard an American Christian as having done his whole duty to God, who renders to his rulers a mere *passive* obedience. If our free institutions are to be accepted as the gift of a merciful Providence, then are all God's people sacredly bound to do all in their power for the conservation and perpetuity of those institutions.

We protest, then, against the course of our "rebel" Christian brethren, on the following grounds:

1. They engaged in a terrible insurrection against civil rulers, to whom, by the most explicit statutes of the New Testament, they were commanded to render honor and obedience.

2. In the prosecution of that insurrection, they perpetrated the most atrocious deeds, or they upheld those who did perpetrate them, and refuse now to hear any rebuke of the offenders—offenders, not merely against the laws of God, but against the instincts of civilized humanity.

3. They not only decline repentance, or to hear any call to repentance, but, glorying in what they have done, they actively persecute every minister whom they can not subsidise, or whose silence in regard to the enormous sin of the late rebellion, they can not command.

4. They aver that this persecution of loyal men, is inflicted on the ground that the persecuted ones "had too much to do with politics," while they actively support and cheerfully and liberally patronize men who fled from the State to the Confederacy or to Canada, that they might more effectively work in this "politics," thus demonstrating, even to themselves, the utter untruthfulness of their averment.

5. By the foregoing proceedings, the churches of the Reformation have repudiated the most fundamental principle to be found in their protest against the divisions of the Christian world—a principle without which the proposed Reformation is an impertinence and a blatant humbug. The principle is this: The whole law of Jesus Christ, as revealed in the New Testament, without addition, and without substraction, is to be taught and enforced, whether the law relate to social and domestic duties, or to the duties of the Christian citizen to the rulers of the State; whether it relate to faith, to baptism, to the remission of sins, to the order of worship in churches, or to any other matter that involves the agency of man. We here affirm, that those who have committed themselves to the theoretical and practical advocacy of this comprehensive

principle, making it the most distinctive element in a great religious movement, do now practically disallow it, in order to shield themselves or their cause from the condemnation of God's law.

May we not, without impropriety, considering the peril to which the very foundations of our plea for reform are being subjected, declare a readiness to meet any champion of modern "prudence," in public debate, on the issues above presented?

In all the churches from the Ohio to the capes of Florida, and from the Potomac to the Rio Grande, the testimony of Jesus against needless insurrection is silenced. No, thanks be to God, this statement is not true. In Kentucky, at least, a considerable body of Methodists have nobly determined to stand by God's truth. They quietly and in some instances, at great cost, withdrew from their brethren, who, as they believed, "walked disorderly." God is with his own truth, and will give them victory. And still again,—forty Presbyterian ministers, constituting the Synod of Kentucky, adhere to the grand, patriotic and Christian Deliverances of the General Assembly, in relation to the sin of needless civil insurrection. Of these forty ministers, is the venerable, heroic, and patriotic Robt. J. Breckinridge, D.D. Who can recall the great services of this eminent minister and man, to the churches, to the state, and to the Republic, in the days of peril through which all have passed, without desiring that it were his, to speak blessings upon him, in the name of the poor and the downtrodden of earth, and in the name of the Lord.

We take heart then, for the testimony of the Bible, on questions involving the very existence of liberty of any kind, is not to be utterly disallowed in Kentucky. It is alleged, however, that, this action of "loyal" Methodists and Presbyterians, has led to schism in their several denominations. Suppose it has, who are the schismatics, those who adhere to the word of the Lord, or those who reject it? For let it be distinctly remembered, that those Christians who remained loyal during all the sad days of trial and darkness did so, in many cases, *for conscience sake*, as well as from patriotic impulses; and they have never hesitated to point their "rebel" brethren to the divine testimony. But who ever heard of any one attempting to prove from the Bible, that he was under obligation to take up arms for the overthrow of the government of the United States? Who?

The churches of the Reformation, congratulate one another on the fact, that no divisions *can* occur among them. This is true, and for the very sufficient reason, that *they never were united.* It is quite an easy thing to have peace among parties that have nothing whatever to do with each other. The "rebel" Christian Churches of Kentucky are united with the loyal churches of other states, about as much as the "Man in the Moon" is united with the Emperor of Mexico; and this boasted union can be mantained, just as long as the parties are kept apart, and no longer. *Individuals* from loyal and from disloyal sections, have met in societies and conventions occasionally since 1860, and it has been with no little difficulty that the radical and *wholly irreconcilable* differences between "loyalty" and "disloyalty," have been so ignored as to prevent disruption in these Societies. All earnest and truly loyal men *feel* that the rebellion was sinful in the very highest degree, whether the parties offending, did so in ignorance or otherwise and much as they may mourn over the evils that have been wrought, and reluctant as they doubtless are to see division, still, they remember that divisions are inevitable until right shall triumph over might, until truth shall triumph over falsehood. For the divisions, those are responsible who depart from, and pervert the ways of the Lord.

We concede the impossibility of dividing the *churches* of the Reformation, for the reasons stated, namely: they never were organically united. But does this prove that the *members* of these churches are united? Our boasting is not wise. But again: *without the most sinful and shameful sacrifice of principles* there can not be real Christian union between those men and women in Kentucky, who, during the progress of the late civil war and after its close, stood by the Bible and their country, and those who disregarded the one, that they might wage war on the other. *Christian union* must be *in truth*, if at all. On naked questions of right and wrong—of truth and error, there can with men of principle be no compromise. "Material interests may be compromised to the utmost, but moral principle can never be compromised—it can only be surrendered." The loyal Christians of Kentucky can "sell out" if they will, but they would do well to remember, that the fruit of the tree of life is not to be obtained by stealth; and that we can neither secure the favor of God, nor promote the welfare of men by hypocrisy. Before there can be Christian union between the two parties to the late civil war, the "rebels" must repent, or the "loyal" men must abandon the most sacred principles. While the actual condition of affairs calls for humiliation and prayer,—the hearty confession of sinfulness on the part of all—the most sorrowing forbearance of all towards all—the indulgence of deep, heart-breaking regrets over what has happened to disturb the harmony of God's people—for consuming anxieties and yearnings for the reunion of hearts—for mournings which nothing but this reunion can stay; yet must we not forget that he who relents toward triumphant and defiant vice, instead of showing mercy thereby, does but betray justice, and truth, and right. Alas, we are in a great strait; "but let us now fall into the hands of the Lord; for his mercies are great; and let us not fall into the hand of man." O, Lord, undertake for us, and send us speedy deliverance out of all our perplexing and sorrow-working complications.

Scattered minorities that cease to be aggressive soon disappear. Those Christians, therefore, who still acquiesce in the justness of our present statements and reflections, will have need of prompt and prayerful activity, if they are to save themselves and their children from the contagion of principles that will prove to be fruitful seeds of innumerable woes to the church, to our country, and to the world. Revolutions and insurrections are born of opinions and theories that can not be refuted by the sword, could we even think it lawful to make the attempt. Free institutions can not be maintained by force—they must stand in the convictions of the people; and in our opinion the perpetuity of our grand and free civilization is to be sought through the Bible and the Church, rather than through political compacts and conventions. Let politicians and statesmen perform their work as they may, unless the church can furnish the state with men who will "obey magistrates and be ready to do every good work," our present social and political organizations must give way. Convictions such as these, may serve to explain our position. We do and suffer for the maintainance of great principles. Do our "prudent" brethren expect that vice will, unopposed, spontaneously correct itself? Where, in universal history, will an instance of such self-resignation be found? No, no;—"evil men and seducers shall wax worse and worse," if left to themselves. We are therefore, charged before God and the Lord Jesus Christ, who shall judge the quick and the dead at his appearing and his kingdom, to preach the word; to be instant in season, *and out of season*; to reprove, rebuke, and exhort with all long suffering and doctrine. God has made the way of the loyal Christian exceedingly plain. It may be, for us here in Kentucky, a very difficult way, but *the true* and the fearless, by God's help, will walk in it.

We may not decline to mention the young people of our State. How have they decided in relation to the rebellion we all have so many reasons to deplore? Ninety per cent of them, we judge, of both sexes, yielding to the solicitations of social success, and to other enticements, have ranged themselves on the side of revolution. This is true of all the young people of the late slave-holding states. The reasons of this fearful fact are obtrusively obvious, and need not be stated. Should not loyal Christians hasten to do what may yet be done, to turn the tide of their young affections toward their whole country, by teaching them that submission to legitimate civil authority is *submission to God?* Unless we can do this, be assured that the poison already infused into their hearts, will, at no distant day, prove the direful spring of innumerable woes to them and to generations after them—woes greater than those through which we have just passed; for, if we are to believe our public journals of all sections, when the floods of civil war shall have swept again over our fair land, it will be as when Sodom and Gomorrah were destroyed by fire and brimstone out of heaven from the Lord. It would be difficult to exaggerate the importance, every way, of this feature of the general subject, or to over-estimate the weight of responsibility now resting on loyal Kentucky Christians. Shall they be found equal to the emergency? or shall "prudence" rule the hour? "Prudence" that keeps "politics out of churches," by alllowing "rebels" to keep every loyal minister out, whose cowardly and carnal compliances have not made him an efficient co-worker with them. We speak plainly, but would not give offense. Men are often deceived concerning their motives, and if this "prudence" is not a device of Satan, he has employed none in modern times.

"Mankind are unco weak,
And little to be trusted,
If self the wavering balance shake,
'Tis rarely right adjusted."

Another consideration demands a passing notice. Is love of one's native land henceforth to be imputed to a man for sin? Is he to be esteemed criminal, in whose heart the flag of his country awakens a generous and patriotic enthusiasm? Must one suffer social ostracism for teaching his children to sing "The Star Spangled Banner?" Are loyal Christians of Kentucky, for the sake of a most false and scandalous pretense of Christian union, to be cut off from all sympathy with what is grand and glorious in our history as a nation, and debarred from any mention of our beautiful and patriotic traditions? Heaven forbid! As a nation we could suffer but one greater loss, namely: the Bible and Protestant Christianity.

Let no man scoff at patriotism, as though it were not a Christian, as well as a mere manly virtue. Out of love of country, which is native to the human soul, God has wrought the grandest results in the history of our race. Beautiful, and even divine is that sentiment which binds the Laplander to his inhospitable abode, and reconciles the Italian to his dwelling place on the trembling sides of Vesuvius. In all climes, amongst all peoples, doubtless, is found the sentiment, if not the song, "There is no place like home." We seriously suspect that the man who affects to like all countries and all peoples equally, really loves none. And does not patriotism show itself even in those through whom God has sent messages to the world? "If I forget thee, O Jerusalem, let my right hand forget her cunning. If I do not remember thee, let my tongue cleave to the roof of my mouth; if I prefer not Jerusalem above my chief joy." Thus sang the captive Jews as they wandered disconsolate "by the rivers of Babylon." For the pious Jew still, there is no land so fair as the land of Jeshurun; no river so beautiful as the Jordan, no mountains so grand as the "mountains round about Jerusalem." It was over Jerusalem too, that Jesus, weeping, uttered that lamentation, which has, we may presume, taken its place among the anthems of the immortals, and for ages past been sung in heaven. Patriotism, be assured, is near akin to the highest form of philanthropy.

We have attempted to discharge our duty—a duty, the heaviest ever before devolved upon us. Right glad should we have been, had some one older and abler taken the cross from our shoulders. It is now to be seen whether or not there remains in our people any fidelity to the principles of both civil and religions action, which they have in various ways professed. For myself, my brethren, may I say, that my hostility to the course pursued by them against whom we this day protest, is uncompromising. I might be willing to die, could this restore the old friendships,—the lost union, the former love; but I humbly trust I *would* die, rather than gamble for place and profit, making truth and righteousness the cards.

Go then, to life's great labors in the fear of God, and in the love of man. While you stand firmly by your most sacred convictions of truth and right, remember that the same authority that ordained obedience to the civil ruler, and in the same document, ordained also, that if your enemy hunger you shall feed him, if he thirst you shall give him drink—that you shall overcome evil with good.

In the language of Kentucky's greatest living son I close; "Every true man must stand in his lot, and do what seems to be his duty in church and state, as God enables him. God is above all, and if he be for us, it is little matter who is against us.

www.ingramcontent.com/pod-product-compliance
Lightning Source LLC
LaVergne TN
LVHW011142110826
845150LV00008B/2472

* 9 7 8 1 4 1 8 1 9 1 9 7 9 *